T0288066

music for mussolini

NOMADIC
PRESS

OAKLAND WORKSPACE
2926 FOOTHILL BOULEVARD #1
OAKLAND, CA 94601

BROOKLYN WORKSPACE
475 KENT AVENUE #302
BROOKLYN, NY 11249

WWW.NOMADICPRESS.ORG

SUBMISSIONS

NOMADIC PRESS WHOLEHEARTEDLY ACCEPTS UNSOLICTED BOOK MANUSCRIPTS,
AS WELL AS PIECES FOR OUR ANNUAL NOMADIC JOURNAL. TO SUBMIT
YOUR WORK, PLEASE VISIT: WWW.NOMADICPRESS.ORG/SUBMISSIONS.

SUBSCRIPTIONS

TO SUBSCRIBE TO OUR ANNUAL JOURNAL, PLEASE SEND AN EMAIL
(SUBJECT: SUBSCRIPTIONS) TO: INFO@NOMADICPRESS.ORG.
$15 (US); $20 (CANADA); $30 (INTERNATIONAL)

DISTRIBUTION

ORDERS BY TRADE BOOKSTORES AND WHOLESALERS:
PLEASE CONTACT SMALL PRESS DISTRIBUTION,
1341 SEVENTH STREET, BERKELEY, CA 94701
SPD@SPDBOOKS.ORG,

(510) 524-1668 / (800) 869-7553 (TOLL FREE)

MISSION STATEMENT

NOMADIC PRESS IS A 501(C)(3) NOT-FOR-PROFIT ORGANIZATION THAT SUPPORTS
THE WORKS OF EMERGING AND ESTABLISHED WRITERS AND ARTISTS. THROUGH
PUBLICATIONS (INCLUDING TRANSLATIONS) AND PERFORMANCES, NOMADIC PRESS
AIMS TO BUILD COMMUNITY AMONG ARTISTS ACROSS DISCIPLINES.

© 2016 BY NICK JOHNSON

ALL RIGHTS RESERVED. NO PART OF THIS BOOK MAY BE REPRODUCED OR
TRANSMITTED IN ANY FORM OR BY ANY MEANS, ELECTRONIC OR MECHANICAL,
WITHOUT WRITTEN PERMISSION FROM THE PUBLISHER. REQUESTS FOR
PERMISSION TO MAKE COPIES OF ANY PART OF THE WORK SHOULD
BE SENT TO PERMISSIONS@NOMADICPRESS.ORG.

THIS BOOK WAS MADE POSSIBLE BY A LOVING COMMUNITY
OF FAMILY AND FRIENDS, OLD AND NEW.

FOR AUTHOR QUESTIONS OR TO BOOK A READING AT YOUR BOOKSTORE,
UNIVERSITY / SCHOOL, OR ALTERNATIVE ESTABLISHMENT, PLEASE SEND
AN EMAIL TO INFO@NOMADICPRESS.ORG.

COVER ARTWORK: "SWEEPING IN WITH THE DAWN" BY MAXINE SOLOMON

BOOK DESIGN BRITTA FITHIAN-ZURN

PUBLISHED BY NOMADIC PRESS, 2926 FOOTHILL BOULEVARD, OAKLAND,
CALIFORNIA, 94601

FIRST PRINTING, 2016

PRINTED IN THE UNITED STATES OF AMERICA

music for mussolini

poems by

nick johnson

for chelsea,
& in memory
of my mother

A poet is always in danger
when he lives too safely,
when everything is deceptively clear to him,
and he is not afraid for people.

—Yevgeny Yevtushenko, *"Love is Always in Danger"*
translated by Arthur Boyars & Simon Franklin

[movements]

la overtura

[poco a poco con tenerezza]

i

[dolente]

ii

[vivacissimo]

iii

[una marcia con il fuoco]

iv

[mesto marziale]

il finale

[pianissimo]

[poco a poco con tenerezza]

chromatic   [i]

oil paint & blueberry pancakes fill the air.
I'm in dad's studio, he's mixing his palette
titanium white — blue — crimson — streams
of orange juice flowing in the kitchen. before
I can sign — he walks away, brush in hand,
lips dancing — I don't know the movements.
he's pushing his brush onto granddad's piano
                          globs of
                    blues
             spill
                    hit the floor
               thump
          fresh morning sunlight
                       like rocks
                 skipping
                       across   sky

chromatic [ii]

this for you— you'll play the piano, he signs,

smiles pushing his brush spreading life over

the keys. I feel mom — her anger on my shoulders.

she's throwing words at dad, heavily they fall

through my fingers. there's a lake on the keys

        change

      burning

   in someone's pocket

      birthday candles

         skates on ice

       an old man's laugh

         singing like saturday

chromatic   [iii]

dad's hands — they find — they — pull
they — hold, he — shares my silence.
mom eyes my fingers' blue — takes me
upstairs, her necklace kissing my back
hair swimming on my shoulders. she
reaches — runs water — rubs the lake
from my hands — dad's signing how
well I played — I can't sign back
my hands muted by mom's — words
under water, spinning down the drain.

chromatic   [iv]

my thoughts pace the room — till the sun
drips under the shade — I hop out of bed —
sneak by mom in her kiss-the-cook apron —
placing pancakes on plates — I hide my bacon
between the stack, pour maple puddles,
each bite crispy, sweet, flowing on a milk river.
dad finishes first, leaves — returns — wraps me
in something — spinning in his warm hands
my smile slides wide — nose catches paint —
fingers find the keys, I push — push harder —
dad pulls the scarf
            lilacs &
                clouds
        cannon-balling
            the lake
                    on my tongue

chromatic   [v]

that's enough piano, signs mom — forcing
the day away on little turtle legs.
I take my cold seat at the dinner table
she's pointing at the piano, her finger
cutting the air — their lips race,
faces wrinkled and red. my spoon and knife,
play, smack, wrestle the table. they hear —
but don't listen. I walk to the piano

   into the forest
      a rumple
     of pine needles
        a basement's
      murky air
     shapes dancing
        in corners

chromatic   [vi]

july outside, christmas eve in my mind,

I can't sleep, the painting's on the wall,

on the ceiling, on the pale green sheets

over my face. I yank them off. slipslide

downstairs. the clock tells me it's 3:21.

I bump a small table — it falls

          a splash

        of the keys

               bubbling the sky

             I leap on

                   sailing

chromatic [vii]

dad cuts my trip short, walks me upstairs
mom's waiting — her hands dart the air
in scattered signs *my father's — god! — why?*
then slowly — *you can't even hear.*
I can — I can — hear the piano — her hand
flies — lands — tears cool my cheek. she
grabs — pulls — we're nose to nose — I
can't tell our tears apart.

chromatic [viii]

I pause at my parents' room tip-toe past
their dreaming — the piano's wrapped
in an old blanket, pushed to the corner.
I get closer, get down, hands and knees,
crawl — unlock wheels. pull, push it home,
the heart of the room, tug the blanket 'til
it warms the floor. turn on the lights.
the keys — scratched, barren — my finger rests
on a tiny smudge where dad had given me
a blue lake.

[dolente]

this darkening

you taught me greek, to speak with your family & we flew
to athens, where they refused to meet me — "o ílios kaíei
kai gia emás 'tous mávrous'— the sun burns for us also,
'the blacks'."

    can you
      tear into
        the night
      like
    paper

                        breathe,

                    fold into it —

renounce
what won't hold
        to the creases

        & let them say

I've darkened you —

§

sitting by the window — she wants to be —
she is — night
seeps in her
morning — she says, the moon
looks like the moon   & stars

 perforate the sky —

        she's trying to believe —

§

a grandchild, she says,
then they'll accept me

when the baby is placed
in their arms —

        will she be their eyes'
        prayer — is even that dark
        foreign   a somali girl

        combing her hair —
        if she were water, what
        color what

        texture — would it be
        a summer
        rain
        puddle

or murky
like a lake
would you wade through

would they
draw
buckets of her

§

              the night
is a child building fortresses
in our branches

— she thinks they will
hold her

§

the lips

the lips that cursed us

the lips that cursed us, on her forehead

§

recoiled hands can extend, she says

tell them — they can hold nightfall,
hold their eyelids shut, embrace it

as if it had bright eyes, a tomorrow, flesh

gathered to smile at them

§

their palms

their palms upturned

their palms upturned holding the warmth of the sun

call it by her name

[vivacissimo]

jazzphorism/
what the saxophone says

be breath or be brief.
            can't
trade me a sentence for a song
            even a parrot
                knows his lines
                    knows
                        words don't hold water.
taste the savory succotash
            I'm layin'
                on these white plates.

jazzphorism/
tête-à-tête

o what, then, have you learned?

                          everything is free.

and how came you to know this?

                          by taking, and taking,
                          and taking.

say the sound of taking.

                          ruffling bible pages, shotgun blast,
                          the register chime.

say again — bibles, shotguns, registers?

                          and tiny fingers
                          caught in machines.

how do you sleep?

                          silk sheets, & dozens of pillows.

jazzphorism/
turn your lights down low

we, gotta be
           economic
      with our affection
love
could breakout,   might
          kink up. conk out.
                 terrorize your tortoise shell.
be afraid of the voodoo you *don't* do
               in a monk's-mood-minute.
          what's rare is precious, *precious*,
so let's keep it few & far between
                these sheets.

jazzphorism/
the current scene

in god
we tryst
    he's
        the company
we keep
   tryin' to save
     we're
       layin' the devil down
in the logo —
      the fine   stitching
       — cotton is   still
king still ivory
  picture it
       — pristine —
   but a funky indigo under
a lumalight
  something's
got to suffer
  for smiles
   to sit
  perfectly
     across lips.

jazzphorism/
slide this in your coat sleeve

only
the slyest fox
eats
every night
&
the brightest
birds always
gonna
taste
the toughest
so
slip a song inside a song
so they'll savor it
seven days
from sunday

jazzphorism/
a human touch

& nimble
    fingers
       to
    knit these
knots —
     & not
        for naught — for
    every
 noose needs a nape
  or is it
every
   nape
   needs
a noose
    either way
       a neck
  is a nuisance

jazzphorism/
the winter of '85

(after romare bearden's collage winter*)*

    a fox

           in a waltz w/ winter

paws

    at the green sky

  in a frozen puddle—

          follow branches

      mother's arms

        train tracks

     a breeze—

  a lick of the ice

          won't tell

       what's locked below

in the season   of the hawk

[una marcia il fuoco]

the manhattan project   [i]

*"placing the center close to the site of the late world trade
 center will not promote healing and as for promoting a
 'better understanding of their religion' it would certainly
 be a constant reminder of the evil it's capable of."*

— *ethel c. fenig*

yes
    we
        are well aware
            of *the evil,*
                the crusades
        done in the name of, felt
            the shackles religion can
    latch onto
        the darkest of us;
            we've
                tasted the *trail of*
                    tears left behind, seen
    what fiendish elation can cum
        when clergymen can
            get a young man to wrap his lips
                around *the word*

the manhattan project   [ii]

a video online — the protest in lower manhattan — seas of
poster-boards stapled to wooden posts *islam is an ideology
a false religion of hate* & I smell burnt oak crucifixes &
I can't hear the old man dressed up in a confederate flag
button-down but he is saying boy he is shouting *nigger*
and the crowd chants *no mosque* but I swear sometimes
they slip in a *no mas no mas no mas mexicanos we're taking
back america* we're doing equations let x be pearl harbor &
y 9/11 and the solution is internment camps not cultural
centers *not on my son's grave*

the manhattan project   [iii]

blood &
      oil in the water —
            stick with the wine.
     ¿no hablan inglés? — we've
got signs against that
              ¿que?
  you —
        out with the old — the
 bring me
     your poor
in with the   *get the fuck out of dodge* — the
hasta la vista, baby — we
 still got little boys
        & fat men missiles
     to knock you
        in your nagasaki —
this is war. we
   stock piles
of people & pyrotechnics
  it looks like fourth of july
            over your country —

manhattan project   [iv]

maybe webster defines terrorism as two planes streaking
through the blue & white day into towers of red-blooded
americans, I am not sure. it is, however, a contract for war,
signed in soot & bent steel. I know its sound, the doorknob
hitting my wall, my pretend-father thundering in my
bedroom like a stormtrooper yanking me out of the night
to take out the trash, or slapping me for stealing his razors
before I knew how to shave myself. it's being black wherever
cops shine their lights or southern gentlemen show off their
sheets; inked against a white backdrop, eyes glance over,
read, define. they want me to believe terrorism is foreign.

the manhattan project   [v]

you talk to the wall
when the light is just so — and in the porous concrete

you see her face.
I'm a rock in their river — you recite this to her

each day your voice
sounding less & less like your own — *my bits*

lining the banks
shining in the sun. don't turn your eyes when

they kill me.
& now you're not sure the words are yours

but they comfort you,
hooded & strapped down, water pouring in, words

spilling out. later
in your cell, you'll rub your hand along the wall

saying, *I'm a rock*
in their river — trying to forget how flesh feels.

[**mesto marziale**]

music for mussolini

there's always an occupation, & a rifle
at someone's back. always a clock & a cross

nailed to the wall, clumped salt in the shaker
& ships on the horizon; be it stars

or starvation, compasses are pointing — embarrassed
by all these bodies undone in the daylight, somewhere

between old testament & tomorrow, you sit on a hill
like li po, your heart swelling like the feet of sisyphus.

§

how the rock offers
pieces of itself to the shore.
            I am studying

what stays.   tracing   with this finger
                the shadows where frames once hung;

what is still with us. which words are we using
these days,   & where can I find them?

the last drop of wine rolls off the glass. you've
said something; I have it written here:

the night lies like hot iron under a hammer.

I took it to mean all the fires are figurative & asked,
how then shall we ever be extinguished?

§

— & there is no telling, but I'm certain
I'd like to be dust

swept from a mausoleum floor.

& often there are days like this, when I wake
in the same body, dressed

in last night's dreams

& what I want the least shimmers
like an earring in the lobe of a lover — & I think

you are the broom pushing

everything out of reach

§

sing me the song you sang one night on the bridge,
over the river, over what you thought was the river

it's all moving. everything's
                aluminum out here.

the world's wrapped
                in its own plastic. the self
unmistakably veiled in its selflessness. wanted nothing
to be all imagined,

                all-encompassing.
wanted only that which could be tucked into a smile
easily given, understood.

write: the river.   write: the river is full of coke cans
                                & there are no horsemen
                                on the horizon.

write this: we have burned all their villages
just to rebuild them.

write this: the poem will not save the poem.

write this: we are smiling in our discontent.

§

he says, *the evening was iced tea*
in his mason jar. & you're

so young you know what he means;
how to talk to him. he's

stretched across the bed— a barge out at sea

wants to be in his chair
remember when his legs worked,

you don't — he wants to watch you run,
skip around like his
                    memory, feel
your steps —

your mother's not even born yet,
how do you explain your existence.

he could hop the hill faster than the mail truck

why can't you, he asks, moving his face
toward the sun   moving his face toward

you — his smile (see it as confirmation)
ignore his shaky hands below the sheet,

eyes reflecting the hospital walls. if only
he could remember he might know, you're not

just one luminous tile
in that sun drenched room of hundreds

§

& now I go to bed drunk as any moon, body
orbiting my heart's sorrow

she comes   only in dreams —
asks   if a soul
          can grow too big for a body.

& if he hurts   the way we hurt

god, I hope so. but I don't know what to say,

          so I tell her   "it's freezing outside;
          aren't you glad you're a snowflake?"

because it sounds something like an answer,
like a koan, because pronouns grow weary

in their skin, dreaming to be more.

she says, *try to laugh a little, son,*
it's all just music for mussolini.

[pianissimo]

tethered

saw them take her
in handcuffs
nude as night   in the back
              of a squad car
        her voice is opal
    the days are hammering
              — heard her
              lost in the coils
      of a rotary phone singing

she says I am sunshine —

she comes home to the same
number of steps, same bed
down the hall, dresser drawers filled
with the same things, she

doesn't look at me directly, says I'm still
glass,

but it's all broken sunshine,
we clear away the debris,

& bleed into who we were

§

was told it wasn't healthy to have your pictures all over my
room

now I see you in a mile of night sky
in photos of myself,

I walked away with nothing,
but a photograph of us,

a snoopy bank full of quarters,
reciting the combination
to the storage container, with each step —

to linger in your chair
& unpack the scent

§

caught her,
ear to the hairdryer, said
the word of god rumbled inside it

said he was calling, she wasn't
ashamed, the way I am

remembering it : the pills
                    the weeks

imagined her singing herself
to sleep the song
she'd sung to me, voice
breaking over like she was a shore

tried, tried to line her coffin
with letters
but the living haunted me

the dead leave stories that keep us
tethered

our guilt to flesh

§

the way a child grips
a photograph

all thumbs & smudges
blurring the image with the thing

grandma died young, so mom
took pictures

vowed I'd have more
than the three she had:

two of grandma standing outside the house
one of grandma lying in her coffin

with each day,
a picture

so I'd have *something*

I spend hours in a photo,
years in the pages

I refuse to fill

§

I think I'd know your voice calling
me in from a window

I'm learning light can shatter a person
or hold them

it took us
a summer

to slip back into our skins,
to relax into an echo of laughter

I'm learning light

grandpa's pockets

(for frank)

summers I spent perched on your lap & sometimes you'd
allow me a search. I'd line my findings along the table:
thimble, coins, a button or two, a peach pit from last spring.
to keep my fingers busy now that the work's dried up.
days were no longer adding up, but carving away,

soon the wind will play me like a flute. you never said
how it would sound.

when the hospital took your pants, they gave you a gown,
a gusty room. we visited every day. I sat close, listened
as decisions were made. when it was time, they placed me
in the hallway, in a cracked vinyl chair, my thumb
and thimbled finger fiddling the peach pit, the buttons;
my pockets singing with you.

the front seat

(for my mother)

when I was 14 they put me in
the front seat of the ambulance —
some things, a child — *a child*
they called me a child —
some things, a child shouldn't see,
kept away like god — confined
to the spaces between pages
viewing the world but not in it
never able to do any thing any one
can point to with any degree
of certainty

      — some things should
   be left
     to mystery
  to magic
a pinch of
     prestidigitation
   & voilà
   now you see
now you don't —
magic, dark magic

what kind of games are we playing here
wait —
    wait —
       it's
          not your turn

they put me
in the front seat
her in the back
she could have lived,
could
    she
      have
       lived
she could've stayed,
could
    she
      have
    stayed

in my arms —

      my arms —

            even if she couldn't

               in my arms

they put me in the front seat, her in the back
with a stranger
that chilled steel box
that unshaven man hunched over
offering her
  a blank
     expression

they put me in the front seat
         I was thinking —
in the blaring quietude of a silent siren
              I was thinking —
waiting patiently at a red light
                  I was thinking —

things
   must not
      be too serious

I
     was waiting
they drew straws
      to   determine
  who
would tell me
        but mine —
mine —
     was the shortest
       mine —
was nonexistent
  I
    lost —

they let me see her with tube tentacles —
they let me see her,
I saw her but it wasn't her
  it
   wasn't
      her —

waiting so much waiting
why is there so much waiting
in death — where is the arrival
I always expect an arrival
I'm looking on streets you've
never walked — in faces I find
I'm listening for your voice
in the rain
I have a tape of your voice
I'm afraid to listen afraid I won't
recognize — I'm

    listening

             your voice

        the rain

             I'm listening

        the rain

your   voice

        I'm listening —

I'm losing. I'm losing you all over again,
memories
    the fading
           rain
     I'm
        listening

I dream you, not often, but I dream you
I can't catch you, but —

each night after
I eat the same meal,
get in bed the same time,
in the same position,
    expecting
           an arrival

they put a man on the moon
but I don't want the moon.
I want a device to record
& playback my dreams

I don't mind eating the same meal,
getting in bed the same time,
the same position
each night, but you're
not there,

          not   there
      in the only
        place
  we
        can meet,
  I don't know why
           you
       keep   falling
     like   rain
              I'm listening

acknowledgments

Many thanks to all the beautiful people who helped
me bring this book into the world, either directly
or indirectly. Chelsea Kirby, you continue to inspire
me and reshape my view of the world, thank you
for your love and support; I am eternally grateful and
blessed to have you in my life. A special thanks to
my brothers Connor Maley and Arun Nagarajan.
Connor much love and a million thanks for your many
reads of this collection; for being my rooftop wine drinking
companion and co-conspirator, and for being the most
amazingly talented writer I have ever
had the great pleasure of knowing. Arun, thank you for
always being in my corner, for your tender words
of encouragement, and for being such a great brother
to this only kid from Baltimore.

Maxine Solomon; your brush amazes me almost as much as
your spirit does. Thank you for lending your beautiful work
to this collection of poems, and for lending your
ear and heart to our friendship.

Many thanks to some of my dearst friends and fellow
artists: Leonard Crosby, Rheea Mukherjee,
Rebekah Bloyd, Joseph Lease, Al Young, Brynn Saito,
John Mann, Phil Lumsden, Chris Carosi, Colin Partch,
Chloé Veylit, Claire Chaffee, Opal Palmer Adisa,
Matt Shears, Victoria DeBlassie, Toyin Odutola, Vivi
Saripanidi, Neil Uzzell, Erin Heath, Frank Weisberg,
Zack Rogow, Sean Labrador Y Manzano, Paul Corman-
Roberts, Patricia Lee, Sarah Bushman, Teresa Walsh,
Jeff Von Ward, and Don Bogen.

& a special, special thanks to all the folks at Nomadic
Press! J.K. Fowler, thank you for believing in this
collection and for ushering it into the world; I cannot
thank you enough. Michaela Mullin, thank you
for your brilliant edits and insightful feedback; this
manuscript needed your eyes and brilliant mind. Britta
Fithian-Zurn, thank you for your great design work.

& many, many thanks to the editors of the following
journals in which some of these poems appeared:

The Cincinnati Review: "chromatic [i]," "chromatic
[ii], "; *Red Light Lit*, Vol. 9: "tethered" (selections);
sPARKLE & bLINK: "jazzphorism/ the winter
of '85," "jazzphorism/slide this in your coat sleeve";
Black Renaissance Noire: "the manhattan project [iv]"
(as "the good book"); *Brilliant Corners*: "jazzphorism/
what the saxophone says," "jazzphorism/turn your
lights down low"; *Metazen*: "grandpa's pockets."
"the manhattan project [i]," "the manhattan project [ii],"
"the manhattan project [iii]," "the manhattan project
[iv]," and "the manhattan project [v]" appeared
in the anthology *Conversations at the Wartime Café:
A Decade of War*.

& my sincerest apologies to anyone I may have
overlooked; I thank you as well.

nick johnson was born near the brackish waters of the Chesapeake
Bay and raised by his single mother in Baltimore, Maryland.
His mother, who died when he was in his early teens, has become
a consistent presence and voice in his work, along with themes
of otherness, and alienation.

johnson received his BA in English from Morgan State University
and his MFA in Creative Writing from the California College
of the Arts, and now lives and works in the Bay Area.

His poems have been featured on KPFA's Rude Awakening,
and have appeared in *The Cincinnati Review, Black Renaissance
Noire, Brilliant Corners, Red Light Lit, Metazen, Samizdat,* and
the anthology *Conversations at the Wartime Café: A Decade of War.*
He is the editor of *Ouroboros*, an anthology of art and literature.

When he's not writing poems he enjoys telling long-winded
stories, Instagraming, making spicy curries, and drinking whiskey;
typically in that order, but not always.